D0902184

NORTH PERCY

by
Paul Goodman

BLACK SPARROW PRESS

Los Angeles   1968

Black Sparrow Press
Post Office Box 25603
Los Angeles, California
90025

for my wife Sally

FOR A YOUNG WIDOW

Playing too happily
on the slippery mountainside
my only son fell down and died.
I taught him to talk honestly
and without stalling come across
but I could not teach him the cowardice
and hesitation necessary
to live a longer life unhappily.

You see, girl, you ought not to
center your affections so,
little short of idolatry.
A young man is untrustworthy.
In the morning satisfied
he gets up from your bed
and in the evening he is dead.

2

His mother and I did our best, Lord,
for Matt, and it was pretty good,
  and he for twenty years gave us
  the chance, without our disappointment or remorse.

But now this leaves us nothing
to blame or regret — only this bawling
  and the bright image that
  around the grave his friends confabulate.

Our prudent Master has begun
us at last to disburden
   of our long cares, Sally, too
   heavy often for me and you

but we did not quit them. Oh
as these things fall away we go
   lighter to our own graves, who are
   burdened also with each other.

4

Where I swim on the gravel beach
  along the smoothly flowing river
the purple joe-pyeweed smells sweet
  the enclosing mountain lowers over

and I am small and safe with my grief.
  Everything is lovely in my home
today when we have little grip on life.
  My little dog stands waiting for me to come.

God of choice, in your real
we two are wandering in hell.
   You know we chose to rear that boy
   rather than to live another way,

when now the corpse blocks the view
what are we supposed to do?
   Too much of us is now a failure
   for us to have a future.

     "Nothing yet awhile."
     Then — mark time march?
     "No, just nothing."
     Halt.

     Shall we break ranks, Captain?
     "Yes, for food and sleep."
     Shall we go back home?
     "Do not yet go back home."

What does it mean when I moan
"I want to go back home"?
"To go back home" here means to die
and this is why I cry.

It means that I am not at home
not where I am nor where I come
nor anywhere that I can go alive
and this is why I cry.

Yet I say "back" as if I knew
and once had such a place, but who
took me away and when was that?
I don't know and it is too late.

Do I imagine when I die
— and this is why I cry —
I will see my son Ready
whom I saw on the stretcher bloody?

7

FOR MY BIRTHDAY, 1967

O God who wear a heavy veil,
I do not need to know what is real,
  yet lead me further where the real is
  although that way is rough. Your mysteries

are probably too hard to live with
at least for me who draw my breath
  short by art and my perverse ideas,
  and now it has been six and fifty years .

PAGAN RITES

Creator Spirit come
by whom
  I say that which is real,
  away to softly steal.

When my only son
fell down and died on Percy mountain
  I began
  to practice magic like a pagan.

Around the open grave we ate
the blueberries that he brought
  from the cloud and we
  buried his bag with his body.

Upon the covered grave
I laid the hawkweed that I love
  that withers fast
  where the mower passed.

I brought also a tiny yellow
flower whose name I do not know,
  to share my ignorance
  with my son. (But since

then I find in the book
it is a kind of shamrock
  Oxalis corniculata,
  Matty, sorrel of the lady.)

Mostly, though, I brought some weed
beautiful but disesteemed,
   plantain or milkweed,
   because we die by the wayside.

I laid my busy forehead
on the withering sod
   to go the journey deep,
   but I could not fall asleep,

I could not rave, I cannot quit
the one scene in the twilight
   that is no longer new yet does
   not pass into what was.

Last night the Pastoral Symphony
of Handel in the key of C
   I played on our piano
   out of tune shrill and slow

because the shepherds were at night
in the field in the starlight
   when music loud and clear
   sang from nowhere.

Will magic and the weeks placate
the soul that in tumbling fright
   fled on August eighth?
   The first flock is flying south

and a black-eyed susan
is livid in the autumn rain
dripping without haste or strain
on the oblong larger than a man.

Creator Spirit come
by whom
I say that which is real
and softly away I steal.

9

This bad world, I induce, is purgatory,
I am not damned but suffer and do learn:
annoyed by flies when I would simply turn
face to the wall and rest, or if I bravely
fight our losing war to set men free,
I gather meaning from it, and I earn
merit as I grow gray — though age is a stern
teacher more than my capacity.

"Is there paradise?" No, no,
I have not heard of anything to hope.
"Purgatory without paradise
has no meaning." But I have no choice:
I do not need to carry my task through,
neither am I free to give it up.

God, thou didst exempt me from original sin
and often with me thy holy spirit doth commune,
    but thou hast plunged me into deep purgatory
    where faith and hope have little substance any more.

I look in the mirror guiltless at my haggard face
and I know that thou hearest my direct address,
    but I do not know how to pray or what to pray for
    and my eyesight is growing dim, thy creature.

THAT MAN AND I

He as wandering he walks
   up to the mailbox
imagines, his mind lapsing,
   that Mathew is living.
Among the steeplebush. I do not dare
   reach to him there,
bereaved are touchy. But I intend
   to leave him behind
with his botany and try what it's like
   on a longer hike.

That man would rather go on
   mourning than his son
be gone for good. This is impractical
   even in dull
Stratford Hollow. I'll go roaming
   among the screaming
cars in the city, carefully
   threading my way.
Let him go crazy
   back there without me.

A day will come when I am dying
   we two again
shall meet. And when we look like strangers
   into each other's
sullen eyes, what shall I say
   and he to me?
when once for all we join
   in absolute bawling,
in the blinding tears that blot
   the world out?

12

Going mad with melancholy
I write the words that make me cry
   — yet let me speak no ill of the
   creator spirit who does not forsake me.

We do not choose the real, she
whispers and I obediently
   write it down, often in horror
   of the things that are.

13

This miner like many another musician
has gradually and oh suddenly
struck a vein of crystals, death.
Plutonic fire was here. I come down
unwillingly into the blazing cave.
My admiration of discovery
has caught a chill from the circumstances.
My voice has no spirit as I speak.

"I will revive Hippolytus,"
said Aesculapius,
"but me, me I cannot revive."
I can revive neither one
but can, Creator Spirit come,
twist the non-being of the once alive
into artificial flowers, and praise
also the never-to-be rose.

I inscribed my last two books
to men alive who were dead
before the books were published.
I was unable to give

these serious little gifts I make
to A. J. Muste and Mathew Ready
who both were warriors of peace
— one was eighty and one was twenty.

Ten millennia and more
men have slain one another
for causes, before I learned
how it is to lose my son.

Do not speak to me of violence
and do not praise to me
guerilla fighters in Bolivia
though I also abhor oppression.

A GRAVESTONE, AUG. 8, 1968

The Sun and the Ocean
and Death are unique,
limiting conditions
within which we live

and there is one single Night
— although De Falla sang
of nights in the Gardens of Spain.
Freedom also

is indivisible.
Its flag is therefore black
not like the other flags
that have armorial bearings.

Come and see, on this granite grout
gravestone is the motto cut
of all the youth of the world:
Twenty Years Unregistered.

Off Route 3 it is,
a few miles north of Groveton,
if you want to know something,
among the orange hawkweed.

17

Ocean, Sexual Desire, and Sun,
and Death, and Flora are the gods for real
that sway my soul, so I freeze, or smile,
or am awestruck. Secretly I often
salute them when I meet them. But the ruin
of my lifetime for the commonweal
I do it as my duty, and I feel
nothing but weariness and indignation.

The Holy Ghost is also my acquaintance
whom I when I encounter sing and dance
with the musicians. But there is one god
for whom I have the others all betrayed,
it is Adam, wasting me for fifty-six
winters in waiting and peace politics.

Our Juggernaut seems to roll
by itself over people
but there are really men
who tend the wheels and engine

only a few hours a day
and jump off and go and play
at home or on the links
and eat well and drink drinks.

Many of them are certainly
much happier than I
and today one came with a poem
that he had made in his free time

(though I am ill I am still willing
to correct the writing of the young)
but I would not talk to him about his poem,
I would not talk about a poem to him.

19

They sentenced David Harris to three years.
He always did remind me of Matty
who was bound that way too, until he died.
Dave is a talker, Matty was quieter
though not shy, and I guess just as stubborn.
They do not grow many as beautiful
among the Americans as those two shaggy boys.
I am sorry for the women who loved them well,
but what shall I say to my country
that has no other use for David Harris?
His day will come, and he will use it better.

WINTER SOLSTICE, 1967

Thee God we praise for the short days
of winter and the instant pause
    of the sun, concealed this morning
    in the unbroken cloud. It is raining
gently on the northeast and we
have brought a dripping Christmas tree
    in, and put the golden star
    on top as every other year

— the golden star and oh the blue
that Matty used to pin below
    to represent Albireo
    the double in Cygnus. There are few
things as beautiful in your creation,
Lord, as this thing that my son
    sought out with his telescope
    and used to pin on our treetop.

I doubt, though it is possible,
dying will be so bad
and I may yet go mad
which they say is horrible,
but probably the worst that can befall
is past me now, Matty being dead.

If he were here he would have hoed
this field where my shoulders fail,
except that he would be in jail
which he and we would cope with as we could:
he was a quiet one but stood
conspicuous and did not quail.

It is a year — I wish that August 8th
were blotted from the diary —
I realize that "dead" means "dead to me"
by now he glitters like a wraith
dim, and my sadness is joining with
much other sadness of humanity.

NOAH'S SONG

What is that lovely rainbow that abides
upon the dripping moments till it fades?
    God promised me, though I am old,
    if I will work this new-washed field

while my future vanishes past,
something will come of it at last.
    This is the rainbow that abides
    on the dripping moments — till it fades.

The beauty of the world
— I still am hungry for it —
to me was always poignant
being in exile,
but since I have no son
it makes my soul sink.

Sally and I are living on
— I see it in her eyes —
it is a kind of bond between us
sure, where much is false.
What a thing it is
to be living on.

I picked a sprig of dogwood
blossoms from the grove
to bring to my pretty home
where we have many flowers,
a kind of bond between us
— I pick them where I wander —

and then we hold each other close
sometimes for an hour
that has no words,
looking at the withering
dogwood from the grove
in our pretty home.

In the variations of the Arietta
molte semplice e cantabile
Beethoven seemed to find it very hard
to bid good-bye to the pianoforte
sent him from London, but kept improvising
rather than leaving off to go about
some other business of dying. He
had had such a long friendship with pianos
and this one was unusually lovely,
its minor seconds were melodious.

FOUR LITTLE PRAYERS

I don't control, daily less,
my any project's circumstances,
    it doesn't happen as I forethought,
    I am trapped where I would not.
But if I let be, as You counsel,
look, it is unbearable,
    my son dead, my daughter ill
    — worse I will not than when I will.

No, it is not amazing, Lord,
that the young I desperately wooed
    and me they paid no regard,
    now greedily around me crowd
to pick at my exhausted love
for wisdom that I do not have
    and still pay no regard to me
    though I am sick, plain to see.

What never was, what cannot be,
what is no longer, are the three
    themes that men invent; and I
    too live on by writing poetry
awhile, talking to You who are
deaf or do not choose to answer.
    Yet I prefer this conversation
    to that of men or women.

Doggedly I dully write
the whispers of the holy spirit
   I hope I do not much distort
   by my misery distraught.
Others have nothing but their sorrow
perhaps — how would I know? —
   but dry and brief is the phrase
   that I say, Lord, Thy praise.

FALL 1968

Eating alone
   apart from the company
because no one
   is interesting to me

and walking alone
   every day
because no one
   will go my way

it is no use
   to withhold criticism
for I cannot choose
   to be stupider than I am.

   Now the year of woe
   since my son died
merges with "I too
   shall die" which always did abide

and this mortal grief
   mixing with
my lonesome life
   and frustrated youth

I am crying because
   the woods are lovely
in this world that was
   not made for me

(nevertheless
    it is good for exile
to live in a place
    that is beautiful)

bitterly because I
    jealously murdered
like the Moor in the play
    her who only murmured

all mixed up is my grief,
    red fall has come
tomorrow I will leave
    for still another home

a man so little
    in touch with folks
ought not to meddle
    in politics

the peace my trouble
    is thirsty for
is too universal.
    It is no wonder
    I do not want power

and victory
    that sits with joy
    on a naive boy
is hateful to me.
    For me there is no way
    but magnanimity.

Surely the destiny
mathematical
to a mind like mine
must be an illusion.

Full of false promise
first weeks away from home
fly by, only later
they drag till I return.

The first year of my exile
dragged, the next went swifter;
though the gnawing pain never ceases
now I have grown inured

to being a second-class
citizen without franchise
who has a foreign accent
I say what is the case.

Oh the first life I shall have lived
in this world has a red sunset,
I shall be reborn
as a braver hunter

as one whose only son
does not fall down North Percy mountain
and bash his brain on a rock.
People will call me Lucky

when we two carry on
the manly conversation
between the father and the son
that we just began.

When Matty was a boy
he used to quarrel and vie,
but I learned much truth
from the quiet youth.

The Northern Crown, nearby Arcturus
in the meadows of the Bear,
for this abstract of stars
in the cold latitude
affirming what is not
I gave my life — see how she shines
in the clamorous night
around my famous head
as staggering I walk
sightless with tears away
from me and my little boy.
I never made this crazy contract
willingly, God.

North Stratford
Fall, 1968

Printed November 1968 in Santa Barbara by Noel Young for the Black Sparrow Press. Design by Barbara Martin. This edition is limited to 1000 copies in paper wrappers; and 250 copies handbound in boards by Earle Gray, numbered and signed by the poet.